FROM A PLACE TO BEHOLD

The Goodman Theatre Stories Collection

Barbara L. McBee

ISBN 978-1-956696-79-0 (paperback)
ISBN 978-1-956696-80-6 (hardcover)
ISBN 978-1-956696-81-3 (digital)

Copyright © 2021 by Barbara L. McBee

All rights reserved. No part of this publication may be reproduced, distributed, or transmitted in any form or by any means, including photocopying, recording, or other electronic or mechanical methods without the prior written permission of the publisher. For permission requests, solicit the publisher via the address below.

Rushmore Press LLC
1 800 460 9188
www.rushmorepress.com

Printed in the United States of America

CONTENTS

Acknowledgment v

Third Culture Enlightenment 1
Decisive moment 8
Inheritance 12
John's Story 14
Le Marais 18
Learning Jazz................................ 22
Letter to Alvin/Making Gumbo 26
Midwest High............................... 31
M 36
Mistaken................................... 41
Pretty 45
Under the branches.......................... 49
Oneness 52
Quilt....................................... 54
The solitude of others 58

ACKNOWLEDGMENT

My deepest appreciation to The Goodman Theatre Chicago family.

Willa Taylor, Walter Director of Education and Engagement, Deb Lewis, Adrian Azevedo, and Liam Collier—for a home to create; to my Monterey, Marin, Martha's Vineyard cheerleaders who comprise my dearest friends: Kathy, Barbara Nell, Kitty.

For Phyllis.

For my mentor Daisaku Ikeda.

May you find great joy from within.

THIRD CULTURE ENLIGHTENMENT

I grew up the daughter of, ultimately, an Army Colonel, whose travels would take me to foreign countries, removed from the civil rights heyday, distant from most blatant racism. I lived a cloistered life, usually the only child of color in my school and in my neighborhood.

I would hear my parents speak in hushed tones about their day. I would decipher the code of spelling words out I didn't understand.

"Is he a 1 or a 2?" Mother would ask of a new arrival or family, or the details of a social or work situation.

"He's a 1," my father would answer in a more hushed dialogue to protect hovering ears.

I searched my minor archives, trying to ascertain what or who a number 1 or 2 could be.

At some point, I would bring a paper to my mother to sign, no envelope; I read it. It was a form given to schools as desegregation came to law asking if you were "black" or "white." "White" was number 1; "black" was number 2. Schools received government monies for having children of color. I lived in the neighborhood, not relocated there, but nonetheless, I discovered I was a designation. I remember the pained look on my father's face as I asked why money was received on my behalf and was I going to receive it? I can't recall the explanation, but I was seven when we returned from Germany in 1962, after almost 4 years.

We flew on one of Pan Am's first international flights—me in my fine coat and little shoes. The flight attendant bent down to speak to me, elegant, dark-haired, slim in her blue uniform.

"Well, hello," she cooed. "Is this your first flight?"

I held my father's hand very seriously. I thought she was beautiful. "Yes, ma'am," I said. "We are leaving Germany to visit my Nana in California." Mom smiled proudly. The captain stood behind the flight attendant. "Well, young lady," she said, "I have a pair of wings for you." She bent down and pinned a pair of silver wings on the collar of my coat. They matched the captain's. I was special.

After one year, in North Carolina, in 1963 or 1964, he would take me on a road trip through the deep south. He explained the history of this country through remnants of filthy colored-only bathrooms, black-only cemeteries, and entire-black neighborhoods I had never seen the likes of.

Mom said, "I'll never use those filthy colored restrooms if I was on my last leg." As years went by, I came to understand that the woods or a pitstop were far better than the options we had travelling in the south.

I was thirsty. The water fountain for colored-only was filled with leaves, rusty. "No," my Dad screamed, "you can't drink from there." I wanted to drink from there, from that fountain, in solidarity with all who stood there, at that evil, that was shat in, spat at, never cleaned or repaired, rusty, and filled with leaves. I vowed never to live in the south. "Florida was as far south as you could get," Dad said. I argued that it was Florida after all, home of oranges, light, sun, and vacations. "Florida is racist," Dad said. "Racist there, too. We will never live in the south."

We were asked to leave a restaurant, hungry, where they refused to serve us. My father stood still, proud, marching erect in his seat, and did not move. I remember because that year, in 1963, I was eating hamburgers in every city and I was looking forward to this one. He ignored the man, watching my face intently, knowing in this crucial moment I was learning something. That waiter served us, then my face lit up at my hamburger. My face fell a little; it was kind of dry, small, thin. I thought it was overcooked, not like the fat juicy ones Dad made. I was sick that night. Mom scrambled among her children. "Ok, Barbara had a hamburger. You won't be eating hamburgers," she shrieked. "Vegetables, vegetables, you're gonna eat vegetables." She clucked over my brother and sister, checking temperatures and tummies. I remember the worried look on my sister's face as I moaned and groaned, nauseous. What I never knew is whether or not my burger was the product of some machination. What I learned was to stand for what you believe is right and just, no matter how difficult.

We traveled to Alaska where I would attend 5th and 6th grade. It was 1964. The mosquitos nearly carried me away, and the bison, confused about the structure in their long-held path, would stare in my window every morning as the herd migrated through. While Dad worked on the Valdez pipeline, I traveled to school by military convoy, big trucks laden with fur and heated generators, the only vehicle that could move through 60 below temperatures and snow mountains. It was a cozy time. I would giggle as strong arms picked me up to nestle me in fur. In the spring, the ground still solid, we waited in line after recess. Behind me stood a large girl. She bent down and whispered in my ear, "Nigger." My entire being responded to the vile hatred in her voice. I spun on tiptoe. I punched her, blacked her eye. She burst into tears, whining, "She started it. Look how she hurt me." The satisfaction of that blow I recall to this day. Teacher snatched us both out of line and sent us home with notes for fighting.

Mom smiled as I presented my note. I was an A student. Her eyes flashed. I stood there. "You were fighting," she said calmly, but I felt her ready to coil. "What is a nigger? I wanted to know." Mom collapsed. "She called you a nigger?" "Yeah, and I punched her." Mom concealed a smile. "It's a not-so-nice word for negro, which means black in Spanish." "I'm not black, I'm brown," I huffed, "and anyway, I punched her because I didn't like her voice. There was hate, poison in her voice." Mom's lips pursed. "No more fighting." I dismissed the word. L was special, smart. My teachers loved me, and always did.

Dad said that a McBee stands up for what they believe, even if I'm the only one in the world who believes it or I would answer to him.

It was 1967, 1968, the height of the civil rights movement, black power, and the Democratic Convention. We moved to Park Forest, Illinois. Dad oversaw Pershing induction center, and prosecuted draft dodgers who ran. It would be over 5 years when I learned that we received death threats each and every day.

I was one of two teens of color in my high school of 2,600 youths. I cut class to sneak into the local mall, with two girlfriends. A car roared by with boys. "Nigger lovers," they yelled.

"Assholes," we screamed. Each of us came to a stop, my friends and I. I . . . I was the nigger. One by one, my girlfriends faded away from me. Suddenly, I was alone, walking home by myself in the middle of the day. I was

14 in my yellow cashmere twin set and red tartan plaid pleated skirt. I was hot, confused, dazed trying to figure out why things suddenly changed. Was it wrong to love me? For what reason?

I came home to ask my mother again what a nigger was. Tight-lipped, she asked me why we were having this conversation. What I didn't know, is that the agent who sold the house to us has suggested we might want to live with "our people." Dad asked exactly who might his people be. The agent had driven him to some project property.

Dad said, "The agent could take his commission or another would." Period. We bought that house, the one that was three stories, with green shutters at the windows, all white. On that winding street where trees were so thick, they created a canopy over it, and when fall came, the streets were golden with autumn leaves that I crunched through on the way home. The first thing I did was hang up a black power poster with a big fist over my bed. My mother was horrified.

I don't recall my mother's explanation but Dad had a way of finding people, sending in FBI, taking jobs, and searching lockers. I never heard that word again. He casually remarked once that the Ku Klux clan used to burn crosses on his yard in South Carolina. I didn't know who the clan was, but I learned that he was fearless, as I was supposed to be.

I learned that though I may have had some privilege, I was viewed as a designation, of lesser value as well, and I have refused to accept that. I am always the little girl with her first pair of wings.

September 18, 2017 c.

DECISIVE MOMENT

It was hand-delivered on a small but ornate silver tray. The card, written in cursive, simply had her name.

This is from the lady. She's standing over there.

It was a semi-formal event, and the tie and vest-clad person disappeared, after nodding to a corner.

She was dark-haired, elegant in a pink tweed Chanel suit, holding champagne. She tipped her glass, eyes twinkling. Her hands were strong, glittering in burgundy polish and impressive gold jewelry.

Are you free to have dinner with me?

She purred, eyes gleaming with intent.

I was intrigued. She really wasn't asking me.

"I like paella. I know the best place in town. Call me. My number's on the back."

She set her glass down and glided away. Great legs, I noticed.

I was curious. And free. I dialed and heard the glee in her voice. She would pick me up. I tore through my closet, determined to match her ease and elegance. I decided on all black…and Italian cashmere tailored slacks and yes, Saint Laurent heels. I knew I would be little more than her accessory.

We arrived at a small Spanish restaurant, and the air was thick with fish and sangria. The table was intimate and she refused menus.

"We'll have paella and keep the wine coming."

Paella takes 30, 40 minutes, for layers of rice and shellfish to be immersed in sauce.

She drank. And she drank. I stopped at two glasses.

She had worked for Howard Hughes once upon a time. She told me of walking the steps to his private jet, life with the girls in the mansion, and his gifts, the first flight attendants, and the people she met.

She drank and drank more. She slugged her wine down like we would have to escape. The paella arrived, fragrant oysters and mussels, frothing on a bed of saffron rice.

Her mascara was beginning to run, and her beauty left her sopping. Drunk. I ordered doggie bags.

She staggered.

"I'll drive."

"No one drives my car."

She was screechy now, her brooch askew, a run in her stocking

We inched across the Oakland Bay Bridge, and I remembered that I could always take a cab home. We poked along the bridge, in the slow lane. She spoke, waving her right hand, slurring her words, weaving as she drove. I don't think she ever left second gear.

When was the last time I went swimming? Could I swim and survive? If I survive this, I'm taking a cab home. I would like to see her house, though. Please get us off this fucking bridge.

The car reeked of wine and sangria.

The blaring police lights blinded me in the back window. She swerved.

Tap tap on the window.

Policeman jolted backward.

"Step out of the car, please."

She failed the sobriety test. She was led away, under the moon, in handcuffs, in her Chanel suit. The police asked if I could drive a stick. I followed in her golden Peugeot, easily shifting gears, to San Francisco's county jail.

I heard her raging from the cells with streetwalkers and addicts.

"Do you know who I am? Don't touch me."

I left her car in the parking lot for her brother and attorney to remand.

I never saw her again.

INHERITANCE

Concrete pushed itself up against where it rang in my chest

Ears tinny my blood boiled perspiration ran down my cheek

My purse slipped

First day in my new chair, my father's chair rolled away

It didn't fit; it wasn't comfortable

I leaned back feeling it for size and fit and settled in

Turning the page on a legacy

You sound like him; he said that he would have done that

Did he tell you that story? I remember. Do you recall?

I don't actually. We were too much alike and when I beat him at chess

From a Place to Behold

He never played me again

I can't understand the rules of cribbage anymore though I read directions

I step up now filling a chair and some shoes that were mine all the time

Too cold for croquet. Does anyone play anymore? Who will play with me?

The yard is snowed in two feet deep and the set waits with the snow-blower

I never use

I have taken his chair and it fits well, rough and solid and prickly

It is my inheritance

JOHN'S STORY

How much is this little chair?

He turned on his heels to face me in my antique store. He fidgeted nervously afraid I would notice the purple red splotches on his throat and jawline.

This is my store….and you can have it.

I shook his hand, to his surprise. I felt the pain in his life, and the surprise that I would touch him.

HIV AIDS was still a mystery, as was its transmission.

Where do you live, because I'll take you and the chair home?

There were tears in his eyes.

His name was John. The person who gave him HIV AIDS was his best friend. She jumped out of a window when he got his diagnosis.

From a Place to Behold

John had never slept with a woman, until then. His friends abandoned him. Only San Francisco General offered any support or experimentation in desperate attempts to find a solution or a cure. He was alone.

I will pick you up every week. First, your doctor's visits, then well have lunch or drive or whatever you like.

Why? He asked me why.

Because I am all you have.

For months, I sat in San Francisco General hearing moans and sighs of mostly men, who were dying and alone.

The protocol at the time, was an attempt to clean blood completely, by machine, recycling it. John would be drained and delicate.

I am willing to be part of whatever it takes to find a cure.

We sat in San Francisco's North Beach. It was a fine day, and the windows opened onto the sidewalk.

We'd like you to leave.

The maître'd and waiter stood at our table. John began to cry.

Our customers don't want you and your friend to give them AIDS.

No one gets HIV AIDS from fucking plates or silverware. I shouted into a room of hostile stares, who turned their backs, forks poised midair.

I bought lunch and spread the blanket on the beach. The waves were easy and the sun brilliant, dappling against the ocean.

A crowd surrounded us.

We'd like you and your sick friend to leave before you contaminate the sand. Their red faces blared cruelty and arrogance.

Again, we packed up and left.

That day, I began to lightly make up John's face before we went out, covering the purple splotches that now splattered across his arms and chest, and further around his jawline. Blush gave him a sense of wellbeing.

For a year, John and I spent a quiet time, taking long day drives to the northern peninsula. He was becoming more and more fragile, struggling to breathe. Sometimes we sat in the car and ate ice cream. It was more and more difficult for John to swallow.

He left me his Billie Holiday collection, on original 78 vinyl, and a silver Lanvin belt.

From a Place to Behold

The phone rang. John had been flown in secret, on a private plane to his sister's convent on the east coast. She hid him and cared for him

He asked me to call you. Please talk to him…just talk.

I prattled on, with reminders of our trips, the latest gossip. His breathing was labored. I could hear him heaving, gurgling.

I heard him take his last breaths. I imagined his sister, holding the phone to his ear, in her habit.

She said he was smiling.

LE MARAIS

Huh . . . deep breathing . . . uh huh huh . . . whew.

I fell outside the door to my tiny room, lugging a huge suitcase up six flights—twelve, if you count each shallow step that doubled each floor.

What was I thinking? What a joke. Next time, I'll pack nothing and fill up my bag when I shop.

I turned the key, sweating, in my mink coat. My first room in Paris. Alone.

"Hi."

Blonde, younger than me, taller, in her dark-brown mink.

"Wait. I'll help you. What's in here? You didn't know? Oh. This is cute. I'll come over. Change your clothes. Let's have coffee."

It was fashion week in Paris, just before New Year's, and it was raining

Bright-faced, Scandinavian, eager.

I threw my clothes into the armoire and gazed into the electric streets. I admired the exposed, dark beams overhead.

She catapulted in my door in jeans; I threw mine on. She grabbed my hand.

"Let's go. I have a fitting later, but there's this cute place nearby and we can practice my English." She giggled.

We bounced down the red carpeted stairs, two at a time, hand in hand, giggling like teenagers.

By day, she ran, fur flying, to the fashion shows. I discovered Camille Claudel, in Rodin's museum, learning she was his inspiration.

I sniffed the great parfums of France and was allowed a backroom tour of one atelier. A drop on my arm, but at 31, I had no fortune for these beauties at thousands of dollars.

We had coffee, black, strong, frothing. She told me what she wore and whom.

Sometimes, at night, she wandered into my little room, after I had staggered in, with some gorgeous Bordeaux and fish on an oyster shell that I bought from a street vendor for one dollar.

"Let's talk. Wanna cuddle? My room is all windows. It's freezing."

She would climb into my little bed and tell me stories of her green home and how she took the train everywhere.

I was charmed by her innocent air.

"Let's cuddle. You like this?"

She blushed. Sometimes, we used our furs for blankets, and I could smell her fragrance, wafting, gently.

"It's my boyfriend's deodorant." She sighed.

I think of him.

My room was lit by moonlight, and the smell of her, her boyfriend's fragrance. Sweet tobacco and herbs. She smelled like sunshine. I imagine he did, too. No wonder she thought of him.

Breakfast, we crashed downstairs down twelve tiny red flights. Bread, crunchy, crispy, and airy at the same time. Butter that smelled like open fields and dark earth. We crunched it in half and slathered butter. The owner loved jazz. Coltrane's longing alto sax set the day as people quickly navigated the cobblestone streets outside, freshly power-washed with lemongrass each morning. I was invigorated.

She went to Yves St. Laurent. I walked to the Montmarte. I peered in at cancan girls and searched for bars where I could girl watch. Paris was filled with models everywhere.

On New Years' eve, the power went out in Paris. I started to rush away, but the shop owner poured me wine and set a beautiful table with cheese. I bought two sweaters and two pair of shoes in the dark by candlelight.

"It always ends," the shopkeeper said. She twirled her necklace.

The night before I left, my young friend brought wine and candles and cheese. I always buy a corkscrew there. We sat cross-legged on my floor. The light flickered in her eyes. I was dazzled by her pure heartedness and how open she was. I commended her to memory without photos. I would return to California with her boyfriend's deodorant in my suitcase, along with his perfume. I left her my corkscrew.

Sometimes, when the light is gray and the sidewalks are soaking wet from the days' storm, I think of her.

LEARNING JAZZ

I grew up in classical music and opera. My mother's mezzo-soprano filled the house, especially when she was happy. She made one 45 before I was born, but she decided to be a mother, ultimately, and follow her career officer husband.

I organized the albums, by letter, by genre. Peggy Lee's album cover of Fever was enthralling, on her knees between swordsmen, I think. I studied ballet, so I lived in the classical section of libraries across the country wherever we were. Dad would tape them and I would organize collections of classical and jazz on reel to reels. I made labels, printing neatly. Sundays when he was home, the house would be filled with music—Mom strumming or fingering on her guitar, a special Spanish one so she could play flamenco.

Dinah, Sarah, Ella, Peggy, Lena, Nina—I understood them, the phrasing of sultry yearning, bop, a quick step, a tongue-in-cheek love song.

From a Place to Behold

I couldn't understand traditional jazz, rattling my nerves, leaving me on edge. I got irritated for some reason, unless it was melodious—Les McCann, or sensuous, Herbie Hancock.

"What's the matter? Too deep for ya?" Dad said.

From that moment, I resolved to learn the language of jazz. I started with Miles, the most complex I had discovered.

I leaned in. I found his pace, his rhythm, his storytelling, his genius, his arrogance. He tells the less obvious story.

Don't play the butter notes. He has told artists who played with him. I took that to mean bread and butter are basics, skip that; find a different entry, another view of the story. I learned to listen again. I studied liner notes. I learned the talk of instruments, how they told the story, describe nature, and conversation even if the writer was less than complimentary about a player. I wanted to hear what they heard or not. I learned jazz was a dialogue I had shut out. I was determined to open deeply to hear what the musician heard and hear his mood and my own.

Was he sketching in reverie with his horn? Did that violin complain, moan in sadness? Was the bass trudging through snow, struggling up mountains, or kicking leaves with each light pluck?

In my early college years, a rogue station took up port at the Oakland Bay Bridge, no commercials, no announcing. He refused to answer his phone to tell us what the song was. We discussed for hours the phrasing, the instruments, the beat, trying to guess the artist. I made a special trip to that little bridge shack and knocked. He never answered, but the music played on.

In my twenties, Dad and I found ourselves slamming back beer in Keystone Corner in San Francisco at Dexter Gordon.

Bzzzzz, the buzzer blared.

"Put your coat on, come down."

"Hi, Dad . . . Wanna come up?"

"Nope. Come down."

Having barreled up from Monterey two hours in his baby blue Volkswagen, twisted with arthritis, we literally sat in front of Dexter's saxophone. He played for me and Dad like no one else was there. I fell in love with Round Midnight. It was a lover, needy, leaning against the door, dropping clothes as they staggered across my floor at sunrise. The moon faded as they carefully slid boots under my bed. Dexter, all six foot 6 of him, hunched over his horn, deep measured breaths, long fingers moving swiftly over his keys. I could hear them softly clack as he played. I applauded, I swooned, I whooped loudly. There is a live recording. I am screaming into Dexter's horn in sheer delight.

We chain-smoked, slammed more pitchers of beer, my Dad and me. He was a Napoleon brandy man. I was never allowed to show up at home without a bottle, so beer was new. I never drank it. I never saw him drink it. But I slugged it down with him, and he bought it. It remains one of my most precious memories of us. Double clutching, gunning his engine, Dad dropped me off as he came, disappearing into the night fog.

October 2018

LETTER TO ALVIN/MAKING GUMBO

Dear Uncle Tubby,

I found one of your books today. Harlem Wrestler. We never talked about this. You, gleaming from the corner in your beret. How was I to know that Domino used to be Domio? That explains it. Everyone knows cousin Fats was really Antoine, right?

Your birthday is coming. It is March, the month of dreamers, poets, shy watchers, and tender hearts. That was you. Dad would say, "Here, here's your Uncle Tubby. Talk to him." We would look, talk about aspirations. Small talk. I was young, working to pay rent, never really thought at the time this would get serious. Someone told me once I had a poet's eyes. Poets gotta eat. That's why you were a professor.

You never forgot the small town that gave you birth. We are Creole, born white, died black, according to the census. Your experience, your focus, was the African root. Maybe, sometimes, the Iberian, French, or Jewish.

From a Place to Behold

You would come to tell the story of the small town of Lutcher, and all that you learned would become mine.

New York Times gave you tribute, with Amiri Baraka who alluded you wrote better. You never made a White House stink, after all, offending Presidents, calling them out for racism. You never changed your name; Alvin Aubert is who you remained. Perhaps you chose to keep your head down while you left history and golden crumbs along the pathway for all of us. Proud of your French descent.

"I know who I am," Uncle Tubby said. I have always said that, living in between two worlds, in a place unique and rarely accepted. Your poems tell the story of my grandmother and my father in Louisiana, a small German town, lumber, and sawmill; of the dead-end street; the boy selling possum in his red wagon; rocks rippling on the river; the boatmaker who made great-grandfather's casket in respect for his nemesis. I imagine the lazy days of simplicity and ease on the Mississippi river—of hard work and gumbo. I have my great-grand's, your mother's recipe. My grand spoke French, as did my great-grand. There was a piano in the house; in generations prior, a violinist. Music surges through my veins like a sprinter in the island heat, pumping, dripping sweat, ceaselessly. You wrote:

And now, in the night

He has come to my room

Barbara L. McBee

He sits on the edge of the bed

Where the mattress sinks

Becomes an abyss and I freeze

There on the edge of it

He speaks. For the first time

I am aware of the moon

It has thrown a grid on his shoulders

Mesh curtains and the moon are on my side

He has come to accuse me

For I have dared to dream his dream

But I am not afraid

I am in league with the moon

And it holds him. 1,1975

Why didn't you tell me my great-grandfather was a poet? His poems were hidden in a drawer, read finally upon his death.

I start the roux, stirring flour until it caramelizes. The shrimp are last, quickest to cook. The smell of andouille sausage browning now, spicy, grainy.

Uncle Raymond gave me the recipe; apparently, no one could unearth your mother's mystery. "The secret is in the file," Raymond said. The day we buried my father, Raymond gave it freely. He was willing, I guess because I really cared—passing on legacy, once again.

Uncle Alvin, you were a watcher. Of course, you were, and together we watched, writing the lives we saw around us, detailing them, the smells, the colors in our heads. We called you Tubby. You liked to bathe in those large galvanized tubs. Did they once hold wine, grain, sawdust? You hid your observations behind warm eyes.

I brown the chicken, adding to the roux, now with sausage and stock, a bit of pepper. I am building a soup like a layer cake. They will marry each other in this ancient Creole recipe from the French, Indian, and African diaspora. You wrote:

Through the open porch window

Past starched curtains

In/thru your immaculate wall mirror

(fixed, ancestral, of its own light)

Barbara L. McBee

men of science read fossils; I read you

I imagine your reply, not knowing

Yet remembering the poet in you; yes

Hold it close to your naked heart; feel

The professor is laid to rest now, leaving behind memories of a small German town, a different time when very little was enough, leaving your trail of poem crumbs for me to follow—how I learn who we are.

I write, I said, in one of our last conversations. You faxed me your complete book list. I understand it now, Tubby.

The shrimp are in last, crab and lobster. I stir, sprinkling sassafras that fills the air with their fruity smell, and I am transported.

January 2019

1. In league with the moon, Alvin Aubert
2. Feeling Through, Alvin Aubert

Both selections from South Louisiana, new and selected poems, 1975-1985

MIDWEST HIGH

You would die for us, wouldn't you, Ms McBee?

Yes, I would. My promise to you when I took this Job…

10, 15 of us were huddled in a stairway, as the alarms rang.

They clutched at me, and each other in fear. No one touched their phones. At that moment I knew they were my sole responsibility. Fire raged in the gym and smoke filled the hallways.

This clarity was a far cry from how I originally felt about the youth in my care.

New people moved to town. Every day, I was scrubbing graffiti off my brick, or bleaching fuck you from my sidewalk. Young girls were astounded that I owned my home. Kids hung on the corners, threw condoms in my yard, and left hot chips packages on my grass. A small group of young girls seemed astounded that I owned the building, peering backwards, they elbowed each other, in admiration.

I pulled up to my house one day to a group of young men, who had surrounded a frightened young girl in my doorway

You think you too good: You're not that cute. Lemme see…lift up your shirt.

Someone made a move to grab her shorts.

I shoved my way into this startled group of boys, and braced myself against her.

Bitch…who is this…. look at this old bitch, like she some badass.

I'd like for you all to just move along…and I will walk you home.

I wrapped her arm into the crook of mine.

You don't have anything to do???? Do you READ??????

The crowd dispersed, snarling, snorting in contempt.

She asked me…. if I read…………

Her mother thanked me…and they moved.

The neighborhood is changing. I want her to be safe.

I decided to tutor in my local high schools. I wanted to offer these youth…. something.

Ms. McBee…. you Indian?

Ms. McBee…. cool shoes

Ms. McBee….no one reads Shakespeare anymore

I put away my teaching plans.

So let's talk about music….

I learned their dances, and related the lyrics of their favorite songs to poetry of ages.

One of my students was always outside somebody's classroom, or in detention. Sitting, just sitting. He strained to listen through the door of the shut classroom, eager to glean something from where he sat, abandoned.

Why are you here… always here?

I can't sit still

His leg jogged up and down, up and down.

They don't like us, Ms. McBee…why don't they like us???

I went to detention and removed him. Next class, I handed him the chalk. He twirled, fidgeted, paced the room.

You gotta move…so……move

He dropped down, did several pushups, two arms, one arm.

Class cheered.

He took the chalkboard, and began to explain. Moving swiftly. Class was in awe.

Every week, he took the board, soon, he wasn't outside the class or in detention. He stopped fidgeting and didn't do pushups. He fingers flew. The rest of the class vied to take the board, and peer teach.

One day the door flew open, slamming against the wall.

I've taught drama for thirty years. That's it. It's over…I may as well just retire. That's it. I'll just leave. I'm not needed anymore.

He was sweaty and agitated, in his tweed and bowtie.

I'm the part time tutor. You are needed here

Ms. McBee…I'm gonna learn Spanish.

Great…then you can learn French, Italian, or Greek… same root

My class no longer laughed at him. I passed detention. He was never there.

He was invited to Alliance Francaise….and got a full ride to college

I learned to Soulja boy…we fought over the best singers of the time. They learned to balance a checkbook, and how to read a map.

There were no more graffiti on my building…. Ms. McBee lives there….

M

She was lean.

Hips jutting forward, one foot, Frye boots, tucked into her lean. A reverse fourth position, thumbs in her front pockets. Her curly damp hair swirled across her forehead, from a bout on the dance floor. Standing behind her, as if in shadow, a stocky, at once ominous, then slightly fearful older woman, flashed me mixed reactions. I made a note. It was like I was watching her debut, but not; invited in, but not. I decided I would invite myself. Maybe that woman was her mother. But lean hip bones would be mine. It felt like two kids under supervision, but not. I was perplexed, and then I just didn't give a damn. I gave her my number.

She was Puerto Rican, the other woman was on again, off again, wealthy, powerful, hoping to send the little bird out of the nest. I would discover this tough older woman was a nefarious drug dealer, though some of her California clients were the finest, and they lived, indeed, in great finery. So, she had trained M that attractions were okay. Indeed, some pretty creative scenarios had

From a Place to Behold

been arranged because the old lady was bored and her youthful toy was just one of a long line of entertainments. The perks, apparently, were no longer good enough.

Maybe I was the one who was supposed to make the old lady come to her senses. Maybe it was because she knew she was headed for prison and the grand life everyone knew was coming to an end; hence, the mixed reaction. At any rate, me and M began.

"I believe in acting on my attractions," M said.

"What does that mean?" I said

"What it means is if I feel like I want someone, I will take them home."

"Um, okay," I agreed, knowing I was a fool. "As long as you come home."

Little did I know I would throw a variety of folk out of my bed, not that we really needed that or that I would be left alone in a private room at the baths, while she demonstrated her prowess in the common room. Once we locked ourselves in the loo in a Castro street haven only to find our breakfast waiting on a tray on the floor outside the door. We were 20 and 23. It was 1974.

We lived on Dolores Street, with one of M's exes and the former husband of that exes' ex, a long-time girlfriend who abandoned them both. His parasail glider took up the length of the flat's hallway. M's ex brought the new girlfriend to live with us. The two rarely surfaced, except for meals, which we cooked together or the girlfriend wailing in agony with severe cramps.

M and I decided to fly to Puerto Rico to visit her grandmother, but when I got there, she said, "Get that *darky* off my lawn."

We went to the beach, now having to spend our money on a hotel that was unplanned. We were stranded. Sad, I kissed her cheek. "We'll figure this out," I said, but I knew this would be ugly.

Dapper Spanish policeman had been parading on horseback up and down the beach. They posted, cantered, tipped their hats, their hand-tooled boots and silver stirrups flashing in the sun. One came to a dead stop as I kissed M's cheek, sand splaying around as his horse spun with the violence of his rein. He began ranting in Spanish, screaming, "Filthy whores. Putas. Get off my beach; putas. Go back to your country. Don't you ever, ever come back here." He screeched, lips twitching in utter contempt, eyes blazing.

We pretended not to understand Spanish while we packed, one eye on the weapon he had now uncovered at his holster. Having exhausted our funds, M's father, a physician, sent us to New York. One-way ticket and a pair of jade earrings for me, to her brother, a medical student.

"One day, M will find a man she loves," he whispered to me, confidently. Startled, I was uncertain what he was saying. During me? After me? Did he think there was no relationship between us?

We flew to New York excited at our luck and it was free. Her brother lived in a condemned building that he wired to live cheaply, independently, while in medical school. He reluctantly accepted my arrival, as I was with M. M and I both got jobs fast, and the plan was to save for an apartment. We moved into a basement space in that same building where I looked up over the black grill at feet walking by. The wind blew New York dust and dirt down into these few raggedy old rooms, with cracked linoleum floors and no toilet. An old metal pot served the purpose.

I came home one day to find M's clothes gone, no note, no trace, and I was alone in New York, with a sleeping bag in the basement of a condemned building, no toilet. I didn't know where she went, or who she might have known. Her brother was finished with me, and I was finished with this adventure.

With the help of strangers who became new friends, I relocated swiftly, a paycheck or two. No time to waste. For five subsequent years, the thought of that abandonment would fill me with murderous rage. As time went by, I worked for a legal firm, editing by day, dancing and drinking by night. One night, as I waited for a cab, I heard the sound of a woman moaning and wailing M's name while she vomited into the street, from the curb where she sat, hunched over, rocking back and forth. I threw her into my cab.

She smelled bloody, wounded, as though sexually violated. I patched her up, tucked her in on my couch. Fearful of me the next morning, I explained that I had arrived in New York with M, and when I saw her throwing up, I brought her here. She told me she loved her, that she would win her back.

I saw M once at a party as I came down a flight of grand stairs. M stood at the bottom. She appeared haggard, ashamed. I found her eyes empty. Not a word, not one of apology. The old woman had given her what she had, and in return, she gave me that emptiness and callousness. I learned never to attempt rescue at risk of myself. I viewed her as if she was under glass, a specimen I must avoid at all costs. I had nothing to say. I thought of choking her, that beautiful neck, and it was gone, a fleeting second. We passed each other as strangers.

MISTAKEN

We were together for only a short time, but she wanted to live in a place we chose together. I loved my apartment with black and white tiny tiles; the bathtub had legs. French doors divided the rooms but we began our hunt. The first stop was Potrero Hill. This apartment sat atop a hill, the first floor, with a courtyard and garden. I was charmed by the view of San Francisco. I took a deep breath and rang the bell where the MD who owned the building was waiting

Would he allow cats? He showed us around where the rooms opened to city views. He wanted a long-term lease. Curly hair, stodgy, tightlipped, he eyed us, first pensively, then a little cold.

I'll make my decision, and get back to you. He snapped his reply. I was certain we'd never hear from him. Credit was good, two good salaries, though we were both in our early twenties. Was it because we were two women?

I have other people to see.

Some days later, the phone rang. Doc, we'll call him, asked me to meet.

We're gonna discuss the apartment. Maybe it wasn't too late. I was excited, planning the boxes I would need to move.

I arrived at a small French restaurant. It was dinner time, 7 pm or so, but it seemed empty. I thought it was a day when it was closed or it wasn't very good.

The maitre'd led me past small tables with lush floral arrangements. Each table held crystal wine glasses for several flights of wine and, oddly, a full staff stood at attention at the back wall

Doc sat alone at a table against the wall. Maitre'd pulled out my chair. I looked around . . . not a person in sight.

Soft violins began to play.

Doc leaned seriously on the table, eyes twinkling. I'm thoroughly confused now and nervous.

The waiter brings menus, places the napkin on my lap, and resets my chair. I shift my eyes cautiously about the floor.

"Oh, it's only us this evening. I've bought every table tonight, so I can talk to you."

My belly bolts. The menu has no prices. I don't understand. I am cautiously optimistic. Are we celebrating a lease? Gosh, what a way to welcome new tenants.

His eyes smile, far from the pensive, tightlipped man who showed us around his apartment for lease.

He is a surgeon, specializing in reconstruction for burns. I might as well order. I am damn perplexed at all this for a rental.

He asks about my life, my work. He doesn't ask about my girlfriend. He doesn't seem to care that I am in corduroys and a sweater, and he is in a beautiful black suit and tie. We have wine, a voluminous, fragrant red. I no longer recall what I ate. Not sure I recalled it then.

The violinists hover nearby. Golly, I adore strings. How did he know French food was my favorite?

I feel guilty eating. Such indulgence wasn't needed if I was signing a lease. How grand if this is how he treats future tenants.

The waiter brings me roses.

What are we doing, Doc? What are we doing? I must ask, now. The food tastes like paper.

I lean back, roses on my lap. He holds his head up, tears in his eyes.

"I fell in love with you on sight."

He sits back.

"You don't know me. I came with my girlfriend, and she isn't just a friend."

"It doesn't matter to me," he chirps. He crossed his legs and linked his fingers.

"We can talk," I offer. "We could even hang out." His work interests me. I might even like him as a pal. He could be a great landlord.

I am a fool.

His face hardens. His fists clench.

"The apartment is not for rent." He snips through his teeth and sits back.

I stand and leave the roses. I shake his hand and he doesn't look at me. I can't remember if there were violins at that moment. In retrospect, there should have been.

Years later, he crossed my research as head of a renowned hospital. Newly married, they met when he did her reconstructive surgery, and he had posted pictures. I was stunned, yet again, she looked like the mirror image of me.

PRETTY

I must be pretty. I never wanted to be because pretty is an insidiously disparaging word used as a weapon against women's intelligence and capability. Pink was our armor, used in death camps to signify gay men, humiliated by being pretty, effeminate.

Effeminate, derived from the word feminine, a slap in the face to most men, meaning marked by an unbecoming delicacy or over refinement, or pretty. My friend, as a toddler, tried to cut his eyelashes off with huge scissors because people called him pretty. He knew it was a bad thing to have these astounding lashes that lilted across his cheeks, caught the sunlight, and fluttered across his green eyes. They had to go. Unbecoming. Delicacy.

I set a transmitter aflame at my radio station because my engineers refused to assist me as the news director. A phone caller said I wouldn't survive, but I commanded an AM/FM station, piloted that hallway between live FM and satellite am, logging miles of pad hours. Stunned they were because I was victorious. Two women asked me if I *really* created a video presentation, if it was *really* me

Got me thinking why they would ask me that question. My IQ wasn't showing, my capability lost in my heels and hair, my femininity. I must be too pretty to get my hands dirty, press a button, battle obstacles, think.

Pretty

Pretty much must be pretty

She's pretty not pretty enough

Too pretty

Not enough prettiness pretty not smart

Good and pretty so pretty

Wanna be pretty

Can't I be pretty

Am I pretty

Do you think I'm pretty pretty is

Pretty does

Pretty good pretty bad

Pretty dress shirt pretty tree pretty shoes

Pretty pretty

Pretty girl pretty boy

Not pretty enough

Pretty but stupid; she was never really very pretty

Wow she is beautiful and smart and lithe and fiendishly stunning

I never wanted to be pretty. I hear the sarcasm roll-off peoples' lips when they use the word—one who suckles, too womanly. Therefore, hasn't got a brain in their head. Has the nerve to breastfeed in public, suckling their children as breasts are used for. You see, people are reminded then, horrified in recognition that this act is womanly pretty. The object of their sarcasm and hatred in full view—an act of defiance against those who have relegated women to their lowest common denominator.

Men generally don't wear pink, so to slap a pink triangle on a man, during death camp days, in a sea of black and gray and stripes, was the ultimate insult. It screamed— pretty, stupid, other, bent. In the animalistic world of the Nazi era, were the pretty wearers of the pink triangle treated even worse than others incarcerated?

If you ask me if I *really* did something that involved thought, strategy, imagination, creativity, time, are you suggesting that my hair gets in the way, that my lipstick stops my very high IQ from functioning, or that I cannot read a manual, that I am too pretty to be capable of anything more than pretty? Why I never wanted to be that? But something must be happening that I am constantly questioned about things that seem elementary to me and are otherwise difficult to others.

Pink pussy hats, the color of my dreams and my childhood, my tutus, my tights and toe shoes, the pink triangle, my Barbie car, and now, a new mission. We took pink back.

Rond de jambe, rond de jambe, plié, plié, oh, Frère Jacques, Frère Jacques, dormez vous, dormez vous, ding ding.

UNDER THE BRANCHES

North Carolina—sweltering, sticky, stinky with the odors of gasoline tar; pine trees, slimy sap oozing down trunks, needles shed, the droopy weight of the branches laying needles in lush camphor at the base of the groves outside our windows. That summer, these weighty trees afforded me solitary refuge.

I climbed them, my gingham pedal pushers on the sharp edges of metal that marked and measured their size or drained their gooiness for science. Perched on high, I surveyed the neighborhood. I read there long novels, Little Women, through several Nancy Drew mysteries. I pondered where babies came from. I was seven or eight years in the world.

My friend's father was a gynecologist. We had bicycled to her house, sauntered into his library, dusky in the afternoon, somber books lined the polished wood walls.

Flinging her blond hair back, her dress starched and buoyant, she drew a leather-bound book from the shelves. We discovered methodical black and whites of missionary positions neither one of us could make head nor tail of. Bored, we rode on.

I got stuck in those trees. Easy to scramble up, deadly heights coming down. I sat for hours.

Do I leap, hoping the lofty needle beds would securely hold me?

Should I crawl down, face forward, into scratchy bark, and buggy nobs?

Barbara Lynn. She admonished me, tickled, amused, having noted my whereabouts and my dilemma from the window.

You got yourself up there, you get yourself down.

It was the end of my climbing days. I was discovered. I took a breath and leaped, catching my calf on the metal bit, just as I bounced on the mattress of sweet needles. The two-inch jagged gash to my left calf slithered crimson. A tidy scar remains in tribute.

Earthbound now, I took to rounding up bundles of fragrant tree offerings, of cone and leaf, bunching them together to form mounds and pathways. I dragged my tea set and Barbies into my new fort and parked their pink convertible in the driveway I carved out.

We read mythology and art, the sun sparkling between leaves that rose high. Fireflies hovered in my little grove, dappling around silently, swinging through, to my delight.

We had tea there, smashed brown and orange caramel corn candies that made me wretch for sugary overload but made a wonderful color for teatime in my cups. We discussed the world as we thought we understood it, the table decorated with cones and splays of pine.

As an offering to the world outside my fort, dad took me to where parachutes lay, on the base, fluffy, voluminous. I learned to fold one, while warm-eyed soldiers stood at attention. I rode in his helicopter. Maybe it was take your daughter to workday. He, on the other hand, spent a large part of the summer in a near full-body cast, his leg jutting out from the bathtub from one of his jumps. My trips outside my pine fort were now relegated to the lapidary shop. We made stuff from rocks I collected from the diggings as I carved out small roadways under the trees.

I learned trees communicate to each other, through roots and leaves, different genus, male and female, reporting injury and season. I often wonder if there is a memory of a little girl who treasured them, building a summer of ease under their branches.

ONENESS

Sit here, she said

These are your people

You come from tailors and jewelers and farmers

One of your grandfathers was

A surgeon general

One grandmother smoked cigars

Two were poets

Another gave speeches around town urging the vote

Who will you be?

Sit down, Socrates said

What will you leave

Behind

Who will you become if you are to better me?

What will you take with you?

What do you leave in your stead?

My lilies arrive after my

Peonies

After the African violets

Leaving the rose of Sharon

And golden oak

Dripping sepia on my doorstep

What will you say if

They rewrite

How the seasons flow

How the moon turned

Because it's not possible

Sit down. Tell me who you are.

QUILT

The quilt lay draped on the end of my grandmother's bed. My Nana was a fierce Texan. She fished, grew her own food, and could hunt and wield a gun like the toughest of men.

She and my grandfather migrated to Monterey after my mom was born where she became a nutritionist on the canneries. Those days, sardines swam in, en masse, and that's what the Italians and Chinese packed when it wasn't tomatoes. Her cookbooks were for hundreds. She taught me to cook, by smell, nose tilted upward, she knew what food needed, or if it was overdone. Fried green tomatoes, hot water cornbread, big pots of oxtail stew, greens, beef tongue, and yes, even chitlings.

A peek in those pots would get a slap on the hand. During the day, we would boil artichokes, eat avocado with a spoon, and crunch on sardines and crackers.

She planted trees—cypress, majestic oak trees that still exist today, towering over two lots, side by side, moss dripping in the fog. Her redwood house was covered in fuchsia and bougainvillea, hanging over the front door. Boxwood hedges brought you to the doorbell along the front walk. The fragrance of that corner brings tears to my eyes and I can smell her tomatoes and weeping willow in the backyard. That weeping willow was my only whipping. I had to pick the branch that wrapped around me and my little brother's calves. Whatever it was, we never did it again. Probably, we were feeding her rabbits.

We would sit for hours in the foggy, damp haze, listing, watching this fishing pole while she dozed. I never saw the fish bite, and I could never figure out how she knew one had arrived. We picked berries in the woods, which became part of her peach cobbler and her upside-down cake.

The backyard always held two or three dogs—Tuffy, the black cocker spaniel, and two others could be boxers or hounds that hunted with my grandfather. There was no petting or socializing with them because when I got through, he said, they were lapdogs. That was bad because they were working dogs.

So, when this quilt showed up in my grandmother's bed—all bows, circles, tidy bits of story, lined in thick cotton, it was a mystery. I never saw that woman sew a stitch or hem anything. I never saw a sewing machine. I never heard her talk about it, or saw her gather scraps for it, but it held my Nana's heart and life and some crazy free time and thoughtfulness that I never saw. She moved back to Texas when she got older. Texas held her roots, and she cooked from scratch, planted pecan trees, and shot rabbits who dared to come into her garden.

"I told that rabbit to stay away from my flowers!"

Mom brought the quilt home when she died, and in her honor, it hangs at the foot of my mother's bed, telling stories in blue gingham and bowtie circles, in blue and plaid.

It turns out, however, the quilt was passed to my mother when she was 18, from my great-grandmother Emma. Emma was a tailor and seamstress living in a small house, on a dirt road, her blond wood floors giving luxuriously with every step in front of her potbelly stove. It was she who salvaged scraps of material, recycled old clothing, and gathered with the neighborhood women to tell stories as they sewed together. When it was time, the women would meet to lay someone's quilt over wood horses, stretching cotton and muslin batting in the center, to sew on the floor together. Emma usually made quilts for twin beds, and this one is a double, making it even more rare. A child brought Emma crepe paper for a school costume, and Emma whipped up something on her sewing machine. I wondered if she used a thimble. The quilt was given to my mother just before she married my father. When I was a baby, it rested on my bed. I remembered it. Little did I know Mom stored it away for when I reached a certain age.

The bowtie is an old symbol. The myth is that quilts were hung out to air and a bowtie secretly communicated to runaway slaves to change clothes, look like you were a freedman, as you made your escape. I have no awareness that Emma was part of the Underground Railroad, and neither she nor my third grand was slaves. Some folks say these are not true stories. Emma and my great-grandfather founded an AME church that still exists over a hundred years old, where both great-grands are buried in the acreage behind it.

The precious quilt's mystery was solved, and I understood the treasure it has become to three generations of women, from my great-grandmother to myself, and I await my turn to see it at the foot of my bed.

In a footnote, per Mom's plan, unknown to me, just ahead of her schedule, it arrived on my birthday this summer, as it is over 65 years old. In every hand stitch, every odd material and color, in pastels and plaids, bright crazy patterns, some with verbiage, I feel my great-grand's life. I wonder what she and her women friends chattered about, as they worked; was it raining, or blistering, soggy Texas humidity?

The card said, "Happy birthday, from your Great-Grandmother, Emma, and, me, your Mother."

April-May 2018

THE SOLITUDE OF OTHERS

What do you mean? You don't know me like that.

I pause from plucking my peony bushes, three of them, two bloomed this year, prolific, smaller than normal. I move slowly in the 90-degree heat.

I don't know what you mean. I just got some hair for my daughter. I got some buttons. You need some buttons? That's all I'm asking. They were two dollars. I'll sell them to ya for a dollar.

I let my shears drop to my side. He meandered through the alley, black teeshirt, and baggy shorts. He was listening to a woman's voice (chastising woman's voice).

I hate that motherfucker.

His head hung as he wandered off slowly, listening closely to his phone.

The protest was a sit-down. White folks protected marchers from the perimeters. A small opening in the street was where they took the mike. Tired of being followed/tired of being chastised, ridiculed, jailed for crimes they never committed. Tired of worrying about their kids. Grandmothers told of days of sorrow, as this necessary thing repeated itself, exploding in the streets in photos and video feeds. Tired of being harassed, promising to keep fighting, to build a better world, where mundane things—a jog, a walk, a beach, a café, school—was a day like any other day. Tired of worrying whether their sons made it home from a trip to the bank.

"This is what democracy looks like," they shouted. Hands up.

"Hands up. Hands up. Who do you serve? You serve us."

"Don't shoot. Don't shoot."

Then it followed—the opportunists, the anarchists, the Aryan nation, shattering glass, shopping for free, with glee.

I got what I could. I got hair for my daughter. That's all. You need some buttons?

Some loot, a woman said, in the street because they never had access and felt they would never ever have the income. Hungry, unemployed, they lash out, taking what they needed, and couldn't afford, taking from where they were never wanted.

Can I help you? Accusing voices berate, not serve, assuming that brown skin means you came to steal, have no right there. You don't belong. You don't belong. Watchful eyes follow you everywhere you walk, everything you touch, leaping to the object, certain it found its way in your pocket, purse, or bookbag.

Determined, if it has not, they continue the stalking. This time will be it. "I'll have an arrest at last for a candy bar, a pair of stockings."

They jump into a sales conversation, confident we can't, won't, aren't able, or ready to buy, pulling away the salesperson who eagerly splits into a mindless conversation elsewhere because they can, forcing us to wait, or leave, or complain if we feel so inspired. This shit ain't new.

This shit ain't new. 1950s. Beautiful uncle Charlie, 16, lanky, rolled his long legs out of the car, getting ready to go to a party with my father and uncles in Los Angeles. Man drove up and jumps out of his car.

"Think I'ma kill me a nigger today."

Uncle Charlie never made it to the party. He bled to death on the way to the hospital. Uncle Alfred was murdered in Texas in the 60s 'cause he was fine, had some money, dared, I mean, dared to go where he pleased. They threw his body on the railroad tracks in Texas.

I faced a gun barrel many times twice because I kissed a girl.

The men on horseback paraded, horses trotted for me spinning, in fine gear on that beach. But I kissed a girl and found a row of guns in my face. They called me whore, told me to go home where I belonged 'cause I was unimpressed by horse trot finery.

I turn from my flowers and remember the stores are closed, as are take-outs, fast food joints, and grocery stores, looted or fearful of looting. No food anywhere for blocks and miles.

I make lunches, packing everything I can for a day or two, for my neighbors, until they can drive to an open market. They are men, they have no way to voice it, teary-eyed, in their pride. It takes pulling, thinking deeply, to ascertain what's wrong, why one is hovering over my flowers. Couldn't say he was hungry.

I am delighted to do something. My neighbors have shoveled snow, painted my fence, pushed my car out of embankments of snow for years.

I make chicken sandwiches. I listen deeply, no judgments. Nothing is open, and his fridge is broken.

What's in the bag?

He peeps in and smiles.

I knew you were sweet. His face lights up like it's Christmas

He won't take the water I offer. I leave something to motivate him to continue, to forge ahead.

Bumblebee circles my snow peas, languid, chubby. It signals the heart of summer, where everything takes refuge in this tree. How I'm feeling now about chicken sandwiches.

June 2020

www.ingramcontent.com/pod-product-compliance
Lightning Source LLC
Chambersburg PA
CBHW021451070526
44577CB00002B/358